NOODLEMANIA!

FOR MY LITTLE MUNCHKINS— IZZIE, TATE, & EMMY

Library of Congress Cataloging in Publication Number: 2012934521
ISBN: 978-1-59474-617-8
Printed in China
Typeset in Franklin Gothic, Hello I Like You, and Mekon
Designed by Sugar
Production management by John J. McGurk

Disclaimer: The recipes in this book involve the use of sharp knives, the stovetop,
and an oven. Children should be careful when preparing, cooking, and baking—adult supervision
and guidance is highly recommended. The author and publisher disclaim all responsibility
for any injury resulting from making the recipes in this book.

Quirk Books
215 Church St.
Philadelphia, PA 19106
quirkbooks.com
10 9 8 7 6 5 4 3 2 1

NOODLEMANIA!
50 PLAYFUL PASTA RECIPES

By **MELISSA BARLOW**

**Photographs by
Zac Williams**

**Illustrations by
Alison Oliver**

QUIRK
BOOKS

Philadelphia

CONTENTS

INTRODUCTION

Welcome to *Noodlemania!* Inside this fun and instructive cookbook, you will find 50 playful pasta recipes, along with neat math facts, cooking tips, and pasta trivia. Let's get cookin'!

NOODLES! NOODLES! NOODLES!

Noodles are a food staple all over the world. They come in hundreds of different shapes and sizes. Did you know that different shapes and types of noodles come from different parts of the world? There are even different colors of noodles. The regular yellowish noodles you see all the time are made with flour, eggs, and water. If you see green noodles, they usually have a little spinach added to them. Orangey-red noodles have tomatoes in them.

Once the dough is made for a noodle, it is rolled out and cut into shapes. The best part about noodles is that they are so easy to prepare. Just boil some water, add a little salt, and drop in your pasta. Voilà! Dinner is done.

PASTA TRIVIA: The first industrial pasta factory in the United States was built in Brooklyn in 1848 by a Frenchman. He spread his spaghetti strands on the roof to dry in the sunshine!

PERFECTLY COOKED NOODLES

Before you start cooking, make sure to ask permission from a parent or other responsible adult. That way, if you need help or have a question, they can be there to lend a hand.

Now, let's get down to business. When you are ready to start cooking, make sure to follow these tips and your noodles will turn out perfectly every time.

1. Always follow the cooking directions on the pasta package. Different shapes and sizes of noodles have different cooking times, so pay careful attention to the instructions.

2. Use cold water when filling the pot to cook the noodles, and make sure your pot is big enough. If the pot is too small, the noodles won't have room to move around when they are cooking and they will stick together.

3. Set your pot on the stovetop and turn the heat to medium-high. To help the water boil faster, cover the pot with a lid. Once the water boils, add salt as directed on your noodle package. Salt makes your noodles taste good, so don't forget to add it.

4. Add the pasta all at once and stir it every couple of minutes to prevent it from clumping together. Cook it, uncovered, according to the time on the noodle package. For a firmer noodle, called "al dente," cook the noodles to the lower end of the suggested cooking time. For extra-tender and soft noodles, cook the noodles for the maximum cooking time. Just don't overcook them or they will become mushy.

5. Once your noodles are done cooking, drain them in a colander. Only rinse the noodles if a recipe tells you to—it is usually done just for cold dishes. If the noodles stick together after they've cooled, you can rinse them quickly in water and then carefully break them apart with your fingers so they are easier to work with.

NOODLES COOKED *AL DENTE* (PRONOUNCED *al-DEN-tay*) literally means "to the tooth." This means the pasta should be slightly firm, with a little bit of bite to the tooth, but still tender.

This book includes vegetables that will need to be washed and cut up for many of the recipes, and meat that will need to be cooked in addition to all of the cooked noodles. Remember to be very careful when using knives, and make sure to let your adult helper know what you are doing. Also remember to wash your hands before you start cooking and again after handling any sort of meat so that you don't contaminate other food items. And above all, remember that things get hot when you are cooking in the kitchen, so **be careful**!

TYPES OF NOODLES

Noodles come in strings, ribbons, twists, curls, tubes, flowers, shells, bow-ties, letters, circles, elbows, and much, much more! You can find many types of noodles at the grocery store or online. You can also buy different colors of pasta, or you can dye them yourself.

To dye your noodles, all you need is liquid food coloring. Just add the food coloring to the water before bringing it to a boil. If you boil the noodles in the water, the result is colorful noodles! The more food coloring you add, the brighter the color will turn out, especially for dark colors like blue, red, or purple. A good rule of thumb is 8 to 10 drops of food coloring. If you want your food to be even brighter, add 1 to 2 tablespoons of vinegar to the boiling water.

On the opposite page is a list of pastas called for to make the recipes in *Noodlemania!* If you don't have the type of pasta called for in a recipe, try one from the substitution chart on page 108.

NOODLES YOUR WAY

The great thing about noodle recipes is that they are easy to mix and match. If a recipe calls for a vegetable or cheese you don't like, use one that you do like. If you don't like broccoli but you love peas, try the peas instead. If you don't like Parmesan cheese, try mozzarella. You can make your noodles however you think you'd like them best.

Now, let's wash our hands and start using our noodles!

ACINI DE PEPE

 ELBOW MACARONI

 ORECCHIETTE

 ROTINI

 ANGEL HAIR

 FARFALLE

 ORZO

 SEA SHELLS

 CELLENTANI

 FIORI

 PENNE

SPAGHETTI

 CHOW MEIN

 FUSILLI

 RADIATORE

 STARS

 CRESTE DI GALLI

 JUMBO SHELLS

 RAMEN

 TORTELLINI

 DITALINI

 LASAGNA

 RAVIOLI

 VERMICELLI

 EGG NOODLES

 MANICOTTI

RIGATONI

 WHEELS

TOTALLY TUBULAR

SUPER STUFFED SLUGS

½ cup ricotta cheese

1 cup cottage cheese

1¼ cups shredded mozzarella cheese, divided

⅓ cup shredded Parmesan cheese

1 egg

¼ teaspoon garlic powder

¾ teaspoon Italian seasoning

1½ cups spaghetti sauce, divided

8 to 10 manicotti noodles

Sliced olives

In a bowl, combine the ricotta, cottage cheese, ½ cup mozzarella, Parmesan, egg, garlic powder, and Italian seasoning.

Spread ½ cup spaghetti sauce in the bottom of a 9-by-13-inch pan. Spoon the cheese mixture into the uncooked manicotti until each noodle is stuffed all the way. Line up the manicotti in the pan on top of the sauce. Spoon the remaining sauce over each manicotti and then sprinkle with the remaining cheese.

Cover with foil and bake at 350 degrees F for 25 to 30 minutes, or until manicotti is tender. Remove foil and bake for 3 to 5 minutes more. Remove from oven and let set for 5 minutes. Before serving, add two sliced olives to each manicotti to make eyes for your stuffed slugs.

MAKES 4 TO 6 SERVINGS

MATH FACT: SIMPLE SUBTRACTION
1¼ CUPS – ½ CUP = ¾ CUP.

CHICKEN CORDON BLUE PASTA

2 cups mini penne

Blue food coloring

1 (15-ounce) jar Alfredo sauce

1 cup cubed cooked ham

1 (12-ounce) can good-quality chicken, drained and broken up

Dash of pepper

6 to 12 slices Swiss cheese

Cook the noodles according to package directions. Drain and return to the pan.

In a mixing bowl, add a few drops of blue food coloring to the Alfredo sauce and stir to combine. Stir the ham, chicken, Alfredo sauce, and pepper into the pan with the noodles. Heat over low heat until warmed through.

Scoop the noodle mixture evenly into 6 ramekins and cover each with a slice or two of cheese, depending on how cheesy you want the final dish to be. Bake at 375 degrees F for 15 to 20 minutes, or until cheese is slightly browned on top.

MAKES 6 SERVINGS

PIZZA PASTA BAKE

- 2 cups rigatoni
- 25 pepperoni slices, quartered
- ¾ cup cooked ground sausage
- ⅓ cup sliced black or green olives
- ½ green bell pepper, chopped
- 1 (6.5-ounce) can sliced mushrooms, drained
- 1½ to 2 cups spaghetti sauce
- 1½ cups shredded mozzarella cheese

MAKES 6 SERVINGS

Cook the noodles according to package directions; drain. Combine the cooked noodles with all of the remaining ingredients except the cheese. Spread the noodle mixture in an 8-by-8-inch pan and top with the cheese. Bake, covered, at 350 degrees F for 30 minutes. Remove cover and bake for 5 minutes more, or until bubbly around the edges. Cut into squares to serve.

ROBOT BITES

1 bag Kraft Homestyle Macaroni & Cheese

Ingredients called for on bag

2 eggs, beaten

1 cup seasoned breadcrumbs

Cut veggies, olives, and pretzels for decorating

Marinara sauce for dipping

MAKES 6 SERVINGS

Prepare the macaroni and cheese as directed but discard the enclosed breadcrumbs. Let cool slightly and then scoop into an 8-inch square or similar size rectangle storage container. Press down to make compact; make the top even and smooth. Refrigerate for 4 to 6 hours or overnight.

Preheat oven to 425 degrees F. Line a cookie sheet with foil and then spray it with nonstick cooking spray. Set aside.

Remove the storage container from the refrigerator and cut the cold mac and cheese into about 8 to 10 squares and circles. Quickly dip and roll each shape in the beaten eggs, making sure all the sides are covered. Roll in the breadcrumbs to coat completely and then place on the prepared cookie sheet. Repeat until all the shapes are coated.

Bake for 10 to 12 minutes, or until slightly sizzling and golden. Remove from oven and cool slightly. Decorate with cut veggies, olives, and pretzels to make your robots. Serve with warm marinara sauce for dipping.

LITTLE LADYBUG SALAD

- **2 cups mini penne**
- **1 (8-ounce) container cherry or grape tomatoes**
- **1 (2.25-ounce) can sliced black olives, drained**
- **¾ cup mini pepperoni slices**
- **¾ to 1 cup Italian salad dressing**
- **3 whole olives, cut in half**

MAKES 4 TO 6 SERVINGS

Cook the pasta according to package directions; drain and rinse with cold water and then let cool completely.

Wash the tomatoes and then set aside 3 of the biggest ones. Cut the rest of the tomatoes into halves or quarters.

In a large bowl, combine the pasta and the cut tomatoes. Add the drained sliced olives, keeping two or three slices out with the reserved tomatoes. Stir in the mini pepperoni. Toss with the dressing and refrigerate until ready to serve.

To make the little ladybugs for your garnish, cut the reserved tomatoes in half. Slide a toothpick lengthwise through the center of each tomato half and then stick an olive half on one end to make the ladybug's head. Cut the reserved olive slices into little pieces to make the "spots" and arrange them on the tomatoes. Place the ladybugs on the salad before serving.

FUN FACT: LADYBUGS ARE OFTEN THOUGHT TO BE SYMBOLS OF GOOD LUCK.

PEAS AND CARROTS, PLEASE

- 2 cups ditalini pasta
- 3 hard-boiled eggs
- ½ cup chopped celery
- 1 to 1½ cups frozen peas and carrots, thawed
- ½ to ¾ cup Miracle Whip
- ½ teaspoon salt
- ⅛ teaspoon black pepper
- Dash of onion powder
- Paprika to garnish

Cook the noodles according to package directions; drain and rinse with cold water and let cool completely. Chop two of the hard-boiled eggs and slice the third.

In a bowl, combine the cooked noodles, celery, peas and carrots, and chopped eggs. Stir in the Miracle Whip, salt, pepper, and onion powder. Place in a serving bowl and then top with the sliced eggs. Sprinkle the paprika over top and serve.

MAKES 4 TO 6 SERVINGS

FUN FACT: DID YOU KNOW PAPRIKA IS A SPICE MADE FROM GRINDING THE DRIED FRUITS OF EITHER BELL PEPPERS OR CHILI PEPPERS?

MIGHTY MAC 'N' CHEESE

2 cups elbow
macaroni

1 tablespoon butter

1 tablespoon flour

¾ cup milk

1½ cups grated
cheddar cheese,
plus more for
garnish

Salt and pepper
to taste

MAKES 4
SERVINGS

Cook the noodles according to package directions; drain and set aside.

In a saucepan, melt the butter over medium heat and then stir in the flour to form a paste. Slowly stir in the milk. Continue stirring until the sauce starts to thicken, about 3 to 5 minutes. Gradually stir in the cheese until melted. Stir the cooked noodles into the cheese sauce until coated. Season with salt and pepper. Sprinkle more cheese over the top to serve.

FUN FACT

NOODLE: (N.) 1. A STRIP, RING, OR TUBE OF PASTA OR A SIMILAR DOUGH. 2. HEAD OR NOGGIN. 3. A STUPID OR SILLY PERSON.

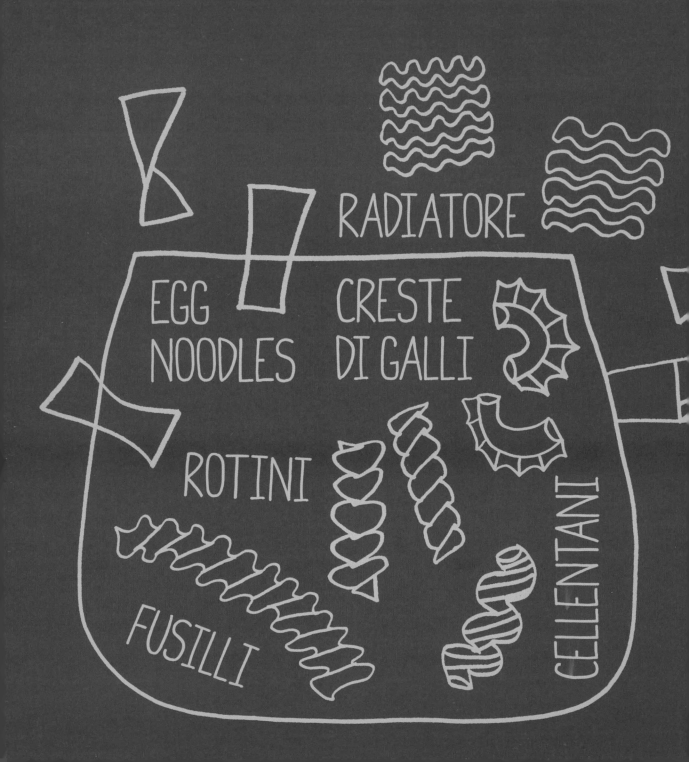

TWISTED & TWIRLY

TOSS 'EM TACOS PASTA

2 cups rotini

½ pound ground beef

1 to 2 tablespoons taco seasoning mix

2 tablespoons water

½ red bell pepper, chopped

½ green bell pepper, chopped

⅔ cup sour cream

3 tablespoons salsa

Shredded cheddar or Mexican-blend cheese

MAKES 4 SERVINGS

Cook the noodles according to package directions; drain and set aside.

In a large frying pan, break up and cook the ground beef until it is completely browned. Drain the oil. Stir in the taco seasoning and water until mixed through. Add the cooked noodles, bell peppers, sour cream, and salsa; toss everything together until well combined. Serve in bowls garnished with a handful of cheese.

BACON RANCH ATTACK

2 cups tricolor rotini

1 cup small broccoli florets

½ cup crumbled bacon

¾ cup shredded medium cheddar cheese

¼ cup salted sunflower seeds

½ cup ranch dressing, plus more to taste

Cook the noodles according to package directions; drain and rinse with cold water and then let cool completely.

In a large bowl, combine the cooked noodles with all of the remaining ingredients. Chill until ready to serve. Add more dressing to moisten if necessary before serving.

MAKES 4 TO 6 SERVINGS

SOMETHIN' FISHY

2 cups egg noodles

1 (5-ounce) can tuna, drained

1 cup frozen peas, thawed

1 (10.75-ounce) can condensed cream of mushroom soup

½ teaspoon onion powder

Salt and pepper to taste

⅓ cup Goldfish crackers, plus extras for garnish

1 tablespoon grated Parmesan cheese

1 tablespoon butter, melted

Cook the noodles according to package directions; drain and set aside. In the pan that you cooked the noodles in, stir together the tuna, peas, and soup. Add the onion powder, salt, and pepper and mix together. Spoon mixture equally into 4 ramekins.

Put the Goldfish crackers in a plastic ziplock bag. Seal the bag and then smash the crackers with your fist until they are all crumbled. Add the cheese to the bag, then reseal it and shake to mix. Pour the melted butter in the bag, and then reseal it and shake until well combined. Put a tablespoon of this mixture over the noodles in each ramekin. Bake at 350 degrees F for 20 minutes. Garnish with a few whole Goldfish crackers and serve.

PASTA TRIVIA: NOODLES WERE TRADITIONALLY EATEN BY HAND.

MAKES 4 SERVINGS

KICKIN' COWBOY PASTA

2 cups radiatore

½ cup cubed cheddar cheese, about ¼-inch pieces

½ cup cubed pepper jack cheese, about ¼-inch pieces

½ red bell pepper, chopped

½ cup black beans, rinsed and drained

1 cup corn

½ cup ranch dressing

3 to 4 tablespoons salsa

1 cup chopped iceberg lettuce or spring mix

4 slices cheese for boot garnish

MAKES 4 SERVINGS

Cook the noodles according to package directions; drain and rinse with cold water and then let cool completely.

In a large bowl, combine the cooked noodles, cubed cheese, bell pepper, beans, and corn. In a small bowl, combine the ranch dressing and salsa. Stir the dressing into the noodle mixture.

Place a quarter of the lettuce on each of four serving plates. Place a scoop of noodle salad on each plate of lettuce. Cut a cowboy boot out of each slice of cheese and place a boot on top of each serving.

GOOEY GREEN NOODLES

2 cups fusilli

½ cup half-and-half

⅓ cup pesto

½ cup shredded mozzarella cheese

Shredded Parmesan cheese

MAKES 2 TO 4 SERVINGS

Cook the noodles according to package directions; drain and set aside.

Heat the half-and-half in a medium saucepan until bubbling. Stir in the pesto and then add the mozzarella cheese. Stir the cooked pasta into the sauce until warmed through. Serve with the Parmesan sprinkled on top.

EASY STROGANOFF SUPPER

½ **pound ground beef**

2 **cups wide egg noodles or rotini**

½ **to 1 cup frozen peas, thawed**

1 **(10.75-ounce) can condensed cream of mushroom soup**

¼ **cup water**

⅓ **to ½ cup sour cream**

Salt and pepper to taste

MAKES 4 SERVINGS

In a frying pan, break up and cook the ground beef until completely browned. Drain the oil.

Cook the noodles according to package directions; drain and set aside. Into the pot with the noodles add the cooked ground beef, peas, condensed soup, and water. Stir over medium-low heat for 2 to 3 minutes, or until warmed through. Stir in the sour cream, salt, and pepper. Stir in the cooked noodles and serve.

GNOME HOME PASTA

- **2 cups radiatore**
- **1 cup cubed deli turkey, about ¼-inch pieces**
- **1 cup cubed sharp cheddar cheese, about ¼-inch pieces**
- **1 cup grape tomatoes, halved**
- **½ cup real bacon crumbles**
- **½ cup ranch dressing, plus more if needed**
- **2 cups chopped iceberg lettuce**
- **1 hard-boiled egg**
- **1 Roma tomato**

MAKES 4 TO 6 SERVINGS

Cook the noodles according to package directions; drain and rinse with cold water and then let cool completely.

In a large bowl, combine the cooked noodles, turkey, cheese, tomatoes, bacon, and ranch dressing. Refrigerate until ready to serve. Just before serving, stir in the lettuce; add more dressing if necessary to moisten.

To make the gnome home for your salad, slice the bottom and top off the hard-boiled egg so that it can stand upright. Place it in the center of the salad; this will be the base of the gnome house. Slice the top third off the Roma tomato and place it on top of the egg to make the roof. Chop the ends of the egg and sprinkle the pieces onto the house.

CURLY WORMS

2 cups cellentani

1 cup cubed cooked ham or deli ham

1 cup cubed sharp cheddar cheese

½ cup olive oil

2 tablespoons Dijon mustard

¾ teaspoon dried dill

Salt and pepper to taste

MAKES 4 TO 6 SERVINGS

Cook the noodles according to package directions; drain and rinse with cold water and then let cool completely.

In a bowl, combine the cooked noodles, ham, and cheese. Refrigerate until ready to serve. In a small bowl, whisk together the oil, mustard, dill, salt, and pepper. Toss the dressing with the noodle mixture just before serving.

Note that this dish is best eaten the day it is made. The oil dressing becomes solid when refrigerated.

COOKING TIP: MAKE YOUR WORMS WITH TWO-TONE NOODLES. COOK HALF THE NOODLES IN WATER WITH BRIGHT ORANGE FOOD COLORING. COOK THE OTHER HALF IN WATER WITH BRIGHT PINK FOOD COLORING.

SEAHORSE SALAD

- **2 cups creste di galli pasta**
- **Blue food coloring**
- **Red food coloring**
- **Vinegar**
- **3 tablespoons butter, melted**
- **Dash of garlic powder**
- **⅓ to ½ cup crumbled feta cheese**
- **⅓ cup thinly sliced spinach, plus more for garnish (optional)**

MAKES 2 TO 4 SERVINGS

Cook the pasta according to package directions. Cook half of the pasta in a pot of water tinted with a few drops of blue food coloring and 2 tablespoons of vinegar. Cook the other half of the pasta in a pot of water tinted with a few drops of red food coloring and 2 tablespoons of vinegar.

Drain the pastas and then combine with the butter and garlic powder. Stir in the cheese and spinach. Set aside to cool.

To garnish, add more spinach to look like seaweed, if desired.

RAMEN

ANGEL HAIR

VERMICELLI

SPAGHETTI

SUPER SKINNY

42
RAPUNZEL NOODLES

44
LITTLE BIRDS' NESTS

46
PURPLE PASTA MONSTER

48
DINOSAUR MOUNTAIN

50
SPAGHETTI AND MINI MEATBALLS

52
SILLY SEA CREATURES

54
PEA-NUTTY NOODLES

56
GREEN MARTIAN NOODLES

58
BEST RAMEN EVER

60
MINI SPAGHETTI PIZZAS

RAPUNZEL NOODLES

1 package spaghetti
lunghi con archetto

4 tablespoons butter

3 tablespoons grated
Parmesan cheese

Cook the pasta according to package directions. Drain noodles and return to the pan. Stir in the butter until it melts. Stir in the cheese to coat and serve.

MAKES 2 TO 4 SERVINGS

PASTA TRIVIA: YOU CAN GET SPAGHETTI LUNGHI CON ARCHETTO IMPORTED FROM ITALY. THESE NOODLES ARE EXTRA LENGTHY—EACH ONE IS 4 FEET LONG!

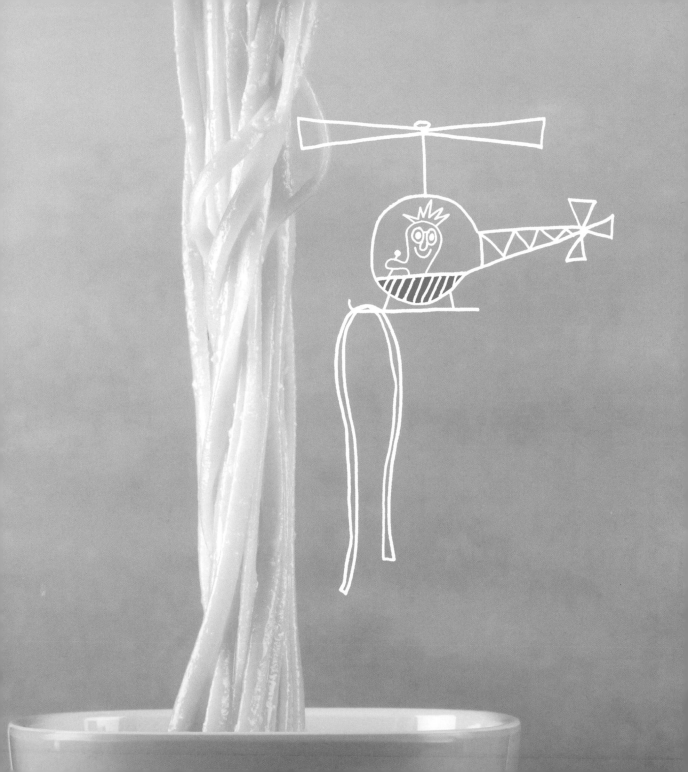

LITTLE BIRDS' NESTS

1 package birds'
nest pasta

4 tablespoons butter,
melted

¼ teaspoon garlic
powder

½ cup shredded
spinach leaves

12 mini fresh
mozzarella balls

MAKES 4
SERVINGS

Cook the pasta according to package directions; drain. Mix melted butter with garlic powder. To serve, drizzle each nest with a little melted butter, top with a little pinch of shredded spinach, and then carefully place fresh mozzarella "eggs" inside.

TIP: YOU CAN SUBSTITUTE THIN SPAGHETTI FOR THE BIRDS' NEST PASTA IF NEEDED. ARRANGE THE COOKED SPAGHETTI INTO NESTLIKE SHAPES.

PURPLE PASTA MONSTER

6 to 8 ounces angel hair pasta

Green food coloring

Vinegar

2 tablespoons butter

2 tablespoons flour

¾ cup milk

¾ cup cream

½ to ¾ cup shredded Parmesan cheese

Dash of pepper

¼ teaspoon garlic powder

Purple food coloring

Whole green olives, pimento-stuffed

MAKES 4 TO 6 SERVINGS

Bring a pot of water with about 10 drops of green food coloring and 1 tablespoon of vinegar to a boil and cook the noodles as directed. While noodles are cooking, prepare the sauce.

In a saucepan, melt the butter over medium to medium-low heat. Stir in the flour until well mixed. Slowly stir in the milk and cream. Continue to stir and cook over medium to medium-low heat until mixture starts to bubble and thicken. Stir in the cheese, pepper, and garlic powder. Once the cheese has mostly melted, stir in the purple food coloring to reach your desired color. Set aside sauce and stir occasionally as you wait for the pasta to cook.

When the noodles are done, drain them and then evenly divide into individual servings. Spoon the purple sauce over the noodles and then top each serving with 2 whole pimento-stuffed green olives to make the monster's eyes.

DINOSAUR MOUNTAIN

12 to 18 dinosaur-
   shaped chicken
   nuggets

8 ounces vermicelli
   or thin spaghetti

1 jar spaghetti sauce

   Shredded Parmesan
   cheese

   Shredded mozzarella
   cheese

MAKES 4 TO 6 SERVINGS

Bake the chicken nuggets according to package directions. While nuggets are baking, cook the noodles according to package directions. In a saucepan, warm the spaghetti sauce.

When everything is cooked as directed, place a "mountain" of noodles on individual plates. Top with the warm sauce and a handful of each type of cheese. Stand 3 of the cooked dinosaur nuggets on top of each mountain.

SPAGHETTI AND MINI MEATBALLS

MINI MEATBALLS

- ½ **pound ground beef**
- ¼ **teaspoon garlic powder**
- ½ **teaspoon Italian seasoning**
- ¼ **cup shredded Parmesan cheese**
- 2 **tablespoons breadcrumbs**
- 1 **egg**

SPAGHETTI

- 1 **package angel hair pasta or spaghetti**
- 1 **jar spaghetti sauce**

MAKES 4 TO 6 SERVINGS

In a bowl, combine all the ingredients for the mini meatballs. Using clean hands, mush everything together to mix it well. Use a teaspoon to scoop the meat to form 18 to 20 mini meatballs. Roll them between your palms to make them round. Cook the meatballs in a frying pan over medium heat until browned on all sides and cooked through.

Cook the pasta according to package directions. Warm the sauce in a medium saucepan. Top each serving of spaghetti with some sauce and arrange a few mini meatballs on top.

FUN FACT: DO YOU KNOW HOW BIG THE WORLD'S LARGEST MEATBALL IS? THE RECORD-BREAKING MEATBALL WAS MADE IN OCTOBER 2011 IN COLUMBUS, OHIO. IT WEIGHED JUST OVER 1,110 POUNDS AND TOOK ALMOST THREE DAYS TO COOK!

SILLY SEA CREATURES

2 to 4 hot dogs,
cut in half

8 to 10 sticks
uncooked spaghetti
per hot dog

Barbecue sauce
or ketchup,
for dipping

MAKES 2 TO 4 SERVINGS

Bring a large pot of salted water to a boil.

While you are waiting for the water to boil, hold a hot dog half in your hand and carefully press 8 to 10 sticks of uncooked spaghetti into it. (Poke the spaghetti into the hot dog, just barely poking it through.) Repeat for all the hot dogs.

Place the spaghetti and hot dogs into the boiling water and cook according to the directions on the spaghetti package. When noodles are done, drain and serve. Serve the sea creatures with barbecue sauce or ketchup on the side for dipping.

PEA-NUTTY NOODLES

2 packages ramen noodles, broken into fourths

1 cup snow pea pods, cut into thirds

½ red bell pepper, thinly sliced

½ cup matchstick carrots

1 cup dry-roasted peanuts

½ to ¾ cup Asian toasted sesame salad dressing

Sliced green onions (optional)

Cook the ramen noodles in boiling water for 2 to 3 minutes, or until tender, and then drain. (Note: Do *not* use the seasoning packet that comes with the noodles.) Rinse noodles in cold water and let cool completely.

In a bowl, combine the noodles with the remaining ingredients. Garnish with green onions, if desired.

FUN FACT: "RAMEN" IS THE JAPANESE PRONUNCIATION OF THE CHINESE CHARACTERS FOR LO MEIN.

MAKES 4 TO 6 SERVINGS

GREEN MARTIAN NOODLES

6 to 8 ounces whole wheat spaghetti

Juice of 1 lime

1 clove garlic

1 large or 2 small ripe avocados, roughly chopped

2 tablespoons olive oil

1 sprig fresh basil (optional)

2 tablespoons sour cream

⅓ to ½ cup shredded Parmesan cheese, plus more to taste

¼ cup thinly sliced green onions (optional)

MAKES 2 TO 4 SERVINGS

Cook the noodles according to package directions. While the noodles are cooking, put the lime juice, garlic, avocado, olive oil, basil (if using), sour cream, and cheese in a food processor or blender. Blend until smooth.

When the noodles are done cooking, drain them and put them back in the pan. Pour the creamy green sauce over the noodles and toss to coat. Serve with more cheese and some green onions (if desired) sprinkled on top.

BEST RAMEN EVER

- **2 packages ramen noodles**
- **1 Polish sausage ring, sliced**
- **½ green bell pepper, sliced**
- **½ red bell pepper, sliced**

MAKES 2 TO 4 SERVINGS

Cook the noodles according to package directions; drain and set aside. In a large frying pan, cook the sausage and peppers together until the sausage slices are slightly browned. Stir in the cooked ramen noodles and toss to combine.

PASTA TRIVIA: NOODLES ARE ONE OF THE WORLD'S MOST POPULAR FOODS, AND SCIENTISTS HAVE FOUND NOODLES DATING BACK 4,000 YEARS. NOW, THOSE ARE SOME OLD NOODLES!

FUN FACT

A DASH IS (A) A SHORT, FAST RACE, (B) A PUNCTUATION MARK, OR (C) A SMALL AMOUNT OF AN INGREDIENT, ABOUT 1/8 TEASPOON. WHICH ONE IS THE CORRECT DEFINITION HERE?

MINI SPAGHETTI PIZZAS

8 ounces spaghetti

2 cups shredded pizza-blend cheese

1¼ cups marinara sauce, divided

Garlic salt (optional)

PIZZA TOPPINGS
Onion, red and green bell pepper, mini or quartered pepperoni slices, cooked ground sausage, green or black olives, mushrooms

MAKES 8 SMALL PIZZAS

Cook the spaghetti according to package directions; drain and let cool slightly. Divide the pasta into 8 sections and then twist each into a layered circle of noodles to make your pizza "dough." Each circle should be about 4 inches in diameter and about 1 inch thick. Line a cookie sheet with foil and spray it with nonstick cooking spray. Place each noodle circle on the prepared cookie sheet.

Sprinkle 2 tablespoons of cheese over each noodle circle and bake at 350 degrees F for 3 to 5 minutes to melt the cheese. Top each noodle circle with a tablespoon or two of marinara sauce, or just divide sauce equally among the spaghetti pizzas. Leave some of the noodle edges showing on each so it looks like pizza dough. Sprinkle a tiny bit of garlic salt over each, if desired, and then sprinkle the remaining cheese over the sauce. Finish your pizza with your favorite toppings. Return the pizzas to the oven and bake for 4 to 5 minutes, or until the cheese has melted and toppings have warmed through.

TORTELLINI

LASAGNA

RAVIOLI

JUMBO PASTA
SHELLS

VERY STUFFED

LASAGNA PINWHEELS

½ **pound ground beef or sausage***

2¾ **cups spaghetti sauce, divided**

1 **cup shredded Italian-blend cheese, divided**

1 **cup ricotta cheese**

½ **teaspoon Italian seasoning**

10 **lasagna noodles, cooked and cooled**

* Leave out the meat for a vegetarian version.

In a frying pan, break up and cook the meat until browned; drain off the oil. Stir 1 cup spaghetti sauce into the cooked meat. Spread ½ cup sauce on the bottom of a 9-by-13-inch pan; set aside.

In a bowl, mix ½ cup of the Italian-blend cheese with the ricotta cheese and Italian seasoning. Spread 2 tablespoons of the cheese mixture over each cooked noodle just more than halfway across. Top with 2 tablespoons of the meat mixture and roll up the noodle, starting with the filling side. Place the rolled noodle seam side down in the pan and top each roll with a couple spoonfuls of the remaining sauce and cheese.

Bake, covered with foil, in an oven preheated to 350 degrees F, for 25 minutes. Carefully remove hot foil and bake for 5 minutes more.

MAKES 4 TO 6 SERVINGS

PASTA TRIVIA: THE AVERAGE AMERICAN EATS ABOUT 20 POUNDS OF PASTA PER YEAR. THE AVERAGE ITALIAN EATS THREE TIMES THAT MUCH!

POPPIN' PIZZA SHELLS

12 to 15 jumbo pasta shells, cooked according to directions and cooled

½ cup mini pepperoni slices

½ cup cooked ground sausage

2 tablespoons chopped canned olives

1½ cups shredded pizza-blend cheese, plus more for topping

1½ cups spaghetti sauce

Shredded Parmesan cheese (optional)

Preheat oven to 350 degrees F. Spray a 9-by-13-inch pan with nonstick cooking spray and set aside. In a bowl combine the pepperoni, sausage, olives, and pizza-blend cheese. Stuff each shell with some of this mixture.

Put the stuffed shells in the prepared pan. Spoon the spaghetti sauce over top, trying to cover each shell evenly. Sprinkle more pizza-blend cheese over top, along with some Parmesan if desired. Bake, covered with foil, for 25 to 30 minutes, or until the cheese is melted and the sauce is bubbling.

COOKING TIP: SOMETIMES SHELLS FALL APART WHEN THEY ARE BOILED, SO COOK A FEW EXTRA. YOU WILL NEED A TOTAL OF 12 TO 15 TO STUFF.

MAKES 4 TO 6 SERVINGS

HOT AND CRISPY RAVIOLI

20 cheese ravioli

3 eggs

¾ cup Italian breadcrumbs

¼ cup grated Parmesan cheese

Marinara sauce for dipping

MAKES 4 SERVINGS

Cook the ravioli according to package directions; drain and let cool slightly. When cool enough to handle, lay each ravioli flat and let dry.

Beat the eggs and set aside. In a bowl, combine the breadcrumbs and Parmesan cheese. Spray a cookie sheet with nonstick cooking spray and set aside.

Dip a ravioli in the egg and gently shake off the excess. Roll in the breadcrumb mixture until completely coated. Place on the prepared cookie sheet. Repeat until all ravioli are coated. Bake at 350 degrees F for 15 to 18 minutes, or until golden brown. Serve with warm marinara sauce.

BAKING TIP: THE RAVIOLI WILL PUFF UP DURING BAKING BUT WILL RETURN TO NORMAL SIZE AFTER THEY COOL A BIT.

SUPER STUFFED MONSTER MOUTHS

Ingredients

1 (8-ounce) bottle taco sauce

½ pound ground beef

2 tablespoons taco seasoning mix

⅓ cup water

1 (8-ounce) can tomato sauce

1 (11-ounce) can Mexicorn, drained

12 to 15 jumbo pasta shells, cooked according to directions and cooled

1 cup shredded Mexican-blend cheese

12 to 15 grape tomatoes, cut in half

MAKES 4 TO 6 SERVINGS

Preheat oven to 375 degrees F. Spray a 9-by-13-inch pan with nonstick cooking spray. Spread 1 to 2 tablespoons of the taco sauce in the bottom of the pan and set aside.

In a large frying pan, break up and cook the meat until it is browned; drain off the oil. Stir in the taco seasoning and water and let the mixture simmer for a few minutes to thicken. Stir in the tomato sauce and half the corn; remove from heat.

Spoon about 2 tablespoons of the filling into each cooked pasta shell. Place stuffed shells in the prepared pan. Top each shell with cheese and then drizzle the remaining taco sauce over all of them. Bake for 18 to 20 minutes, or until cheese is melted and sauce is bubbling.

To serve, use toothpicks to stick two tomato halves onto each shell to make eyes. (Remove the toothpicks before eating!) Make teeth by placing pieces of corn along the edges of each shell to make a monster mouth.

TOTEM POLE TORTELLINI

- 10 large or 20 small bamboo skewers
- 4 ounces sharp cheddar cheese, cut into about 20 cubes
- 4 ounces Monterey Jack cheese, cut into about 20 cubes
- 2 cups rainbow cheese tortellini, cooked and cooled
- 20 grape or small cherry tomatoes
- 20 whole black or green olives
- ¼ cup Italian salad dressing for serving

FOR TOTEM POLE FACES
shredded purple cabbage, matchstick carrots, red and green bell peppers, green onions, capers, shredded wheat

Make "totem poles" by arranging cheese cubes, tortellini, tomatoes, and olives on each skewer. Brush dressing over kabobs before decorating.

Using another bamboo skewer to poke holes, add hair made of shredded purple cabbage, matchstick carrots, the dark-green ends of green onions, or shredded wheat. Arrange olives or capers to look like eyes. Make mouths out of pieces of bell pepper or carrot. Go crazy!

MAKES 20 SMALL OR 10 LARGE KABOBS

ROLLIN' CHICKEN ALFREDO

1 (15-ounce) jar
Alfredo sauce,
divided

1½ cups Italian-blend
cheese, divided

1¼ cups ricotta cheese

½ teaspoon Italian
seasoning

1 egg

Salt and pepper

1 to 2 cups chopped
rotisserie chicken*

10 lasagna noodles,
cooked according
to directions and
cooled

* 1 (12-ounce) can
good-quality
chicken may be
substituted.

Spray a 9-by-13-inch pan with nonstick cooking spray. Spread about ½ cup of the Alfredo sauce on the bottom of the pan; set aside.

In a bowl, mix ½ cup of the Italian-blend cheese with the ricotta cheese, Italian seasoning, egg, and salt and pepper. Spread 2 heaping tablespoons of the cheese mixture over each noodle just more than halfway across. Top with 2 tablespoons chicken. Roll up the noodle, starting with the filling side.

Place each noodle roll seam side down in the prepared pan. Top each roll with a couple spoonfuls of the remaining sauce and cheese. Preheat oven to 350 degrees F and bake, covered with foil, for 25 minutes. Carefully remove hot foil and bake for 5 minutes more.

MAKES 4 TO
6 SERVINGS

TORTELLINI SOUP

½ cup sliced carrots

½ cup sliced celery

4 cups chicken broth

Dash of onion powder

Dash of ground thyme

Dash of pepper

2 cups rainbow cheese tortellini

1 (12-ounce) can of good-quality chicken, drained and broken up

In a soup pot, combine the carrots, celery, chicken broth, onion powder, thyme, and pepper. Bring to a low boil and let cook for about 3 to 5 minutes. Add the tortellini and cook for about 6 to 8 minutes more, or until the pasta is tender. Stir in the chicken just before the pasta is done cooking and heat through.

MAKES 4 TO 6 SERVINGS

BIG FAT CHEESY SHELLS

- **12 to 15 jumbo pasta shells**
- **½ cup ricotta cheese**
- **1¼ cups shredded mozzarella cheese, divided**
- **½ cup grated Parmesan cheese**
- **1 egg**
- **½ tablespoon dried parsley**
- **1¼ cups marinara sauce**

MAKES 4 TO
6 SERVINGS

Cook the pasta according to package directions and set aside to cool.

In a bowl, combine the ricotta cheese, ½ cup of the mozzarella cheese, Parmesan cheese, egg, and parsley. Scoop the cheese mixture evenly into the cooked shells.

Spray a 9-by-13-inch baking dish with nonstick cooking spray. Spread about ⅓ cup of the marinara sauce in the bottom of the pan. Place the stuffed shells in the pan. Spoon the remaining sauce over each shell to cover. Sprinkle the remaining mozzarella cheese over top. Preheat oven to 350 degrees F and bake, covered with foil, for 30 minutes.

RAVIOLI CUPCAKES

1¼ cups spaghetti sauce

12 large cheese ravioli, from refrigerated section of grocery store

½ pound ground beef, cooked and drained

1¼ cups grated mozzarella cheese

¼ cup Parmesan cheese

MAKES 6 SERVINGS

Preheat oven to 350 degrees F. Spray a 6-cup jumbo muffin tin with nonstick cooking spray. Place a spoonful of spaghetti sauce in the bottom of each cup. Then top with a ravioli, 1 tablespoon of the meat, and a spoonful of sauce. Sprinkle with 1 tablespoon of mozzarella cheese. Repeat the layers. Top each cup with any remaining mozzarella and Parmesan cheese. Bake for 30 minutes, or until the "cupcakes" are bubbling around the edges.

COOKING TIP: IF YOU DON'T HAVE A JUMBO MUFFIN TIN, USE A REGULAR MUFFIN TIN AND SUBSTITUTE SMALLER RAVIOLI.

HOMEMADE PASTA

1 cup flour
½ teaspoon salt
1 egg, slightly beaten
1 to 2 tablespoons water

MAKES 6 SERVINGS

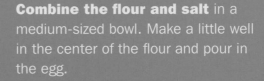

Combine the flour and salt in a medium-sized bowl. Make a little well in the center of the flour and pour in the egg.

Mix until it forms a stiff dough. Add 1 to 2 tablespoons of water if needed.

On a lightly floured surface, knead the dough with your hands for about 3 minutes. Then roll it out until it is about ⅛ inch thick. Use a butter knife to cut it into thin strips.

Cook according to your favorite recipe and enjoy!

Note: This dough has egg in it, so cook right away or keep in the refrigerator for a day or two before using.

BOW-TIE

STARS

ORZO

MINI FARFALLE

RIGATONI

ROTINI

ORECCHIETTE

FUSILLI

FIORI

WHEELS

SEA SHELL

CHOW MEIN

WHEELS & WHATEVER

ROBOT PARTS

2½ cups assorted pasta (such as rotini, fusilli, wheels, mini farfalle, rigatoni)

Food coloring

Vinegar

1 can black olives

½ cucumber, sliced

1 cup Italian salad dressing

¾ cup grated Parmesan cheese

MAKES 4 TO 6 SERVINGS

Cook the pasta according to package directions. Cook in several different pots with water tinted with different colors of food coloring, as desired; to each pot of colored water, add a few drops of vinegar. Rinse the noodles and let cool. Combine the different pastas and toss them with the olives, cucumber, salad dressing, and Parmesan cheese.

VARIATION: AFTER COOKING PASTA, SERVE HOT WITH MARINARA SAUCE AND TOP WITH PARMESAN CHEESE. OMIT OTHER INGREDIENTS.

BBQ BIRD

2 cups wheels pasta

2 cups cut-up rotisserie chicken

1 cup frozen super-sweet petite corn, thawed

1 cup barbecue sauce

2 cups bagged coleslaw salad mix

¼ cup ranch dressing

1 green onion, sliced (optional)

Shredded extra-sharp white cheddar cheese

MAKES 4 TO 6 SERVINGS

Cook the noodles according to package directions and then drain and set aside. Put the chicken, corn, and barbecue sauce in a large saucepan and heat through. In a bowl, toss the coleslaw mix with the ranch dressing and half of the green onion slices, if using.

Gently stir the noodles into the chicken mixture. Scoop some coleslaw onto a plate and then top with a large scoop of the barbecue chicken and noodles. Garnish with the white cheddar cheese and a little green onion.

PINK PEPPERONI FLOWERS

½ pound sausage
2 cups fiori pasta
1½ cups marinara sauce
⅓ cup heavy cream
Shredded mozzarella cheese
6 pepperoni slices
6 slices of green or black olive

MAKES 6 SERVINGS

In a frying pan, break apart and cook the sausage until it is browned; drain the fat. Cook the noodles according to package directions; drain and let cool.

While the noodles cool, add the marinara sauce to the sausage in the frying pan and heat through. Stir in the cream until well combined. Stir in the noodles. Divide the noodle mixture evenly among 6 ramekins and top each with 1 or 2 tablespoons of mozzarella cheese.

Set the pepperoni on a cutting board and use a small flower-shaped cookie cutter to cut each slice into a flower. Place a pepperoni flower on top of each noodle dish. Top with an olive slice stuffed with a little mozzarella, if desired, to make the flower center. Bake at 350 degrees F for 5 minutes, or until cheese is melted.

UNDER THE CHEESY SEA SHELLS

1½ cups small
    seashell pasta

   Blue food coloring

   Vinegar

⅓ cup 2 percent or
    whole milk

 3 to 4 tablespoons
    Old English cheese
    spread

   Dash of garlic salt

 4 cooked hot dogs

   Mustard

MAKES 4 SERVINGS

Cook the noodles according to package directions, adding a few drops of blue food coloring and 1 to 2 tablespoons of vinegar to the cooking water. Drain and return the noodles to the pan. In a separate pan, stir the milk and cheese spread until smooth. Season with the garlic salt and stir to combine.

To make an octopus, cut each hot dog in half lengthwise only to the middle. Then cut each half in half again so there are 4 tentacles. Repeat a third time to make 8 tentacles.

To serve, place the seashell noodles in a serving bowl. Pour the sauce over the top. Place your octopus on top of individual servings of noodles. Place two dots of mustard on each octopus to make the eyes.

PASTA TRIVIA: CHEESE IS THE INGREDIENT MOST COMMONLY MIXED IN WITH NOODLES.

"I'M SO BLUE" HULA HAYSTACKS

1 cup uncooked rice

2 cups water

Salt to taste

3 to 4 drops blue food coloring

1 (10.75-ounce) can condensed cream of chicken soup

½ soup can of milk

1 (12-ounce) can good-quality chicken, drained

½ cup sour cream

Dash of pepper

1 cup grated cheddar cheese

1 cup chow mein noodles

TOPPINGS
chopped celery, peas, pineapple tidbits, sliced green onion, matchstick carrots, diced bell peppers, chopped tomatoes

Put the rice, water, salt, and food coloring in a pan with a lid and stir. Bring to a boil and then turn down the heat to low and cover with the lid. Let cook for 15 minutes and then fluff the rice with a spoon or fork.

While the rice is cooking, combine the soup with the milk and chicken in a saucepan and heat through. Just before you are ready to serve, stir in the sour cream and pepper and heat through. Serve in individual bowls over the blue rice and top with the cheese and chow mein noodles. Let everyone add favorite toppings.

MAKES 4 TO 6 SERVINGS

OVER-THE-RAINBOW SALAD

2 cups rainbow bow-tie pasta

½ cup chopped celery

½ cup frozen peas, thawed

1 cup spinach, coarsely chopped

½ cup Caesar salad dressing, plus more if desired

⅓ cup shredded Asiago cheese

MAKES 6 SERVINGS

Cook the noodles according to package directions; drain and rinse with cold water and then let cool completely. Toss together the cooled noodles, celery, peas, and spinach with the salad dressing and cheese. Refrigerate until ready to serve. Add more dressing to moisten if needed.

COOKING TIP: YOU CAN USE ANY BOW-TIE PASTA FOR THIS RECIPE, BUT THE RAINBOW BOW-TIE PASTA THAT YOU CAN BUY ONLINE IS REALLY FUN!

OUT-OF-THIS-WORLD TOMATO SOUP

- **1 family-sized can condensed tomato soup**
- **1 soup can of water**
- **1 teaspoon dried basil**
- **¼ teaspoon garlic powder**
- **¾ cup star noodles**

MAKES 4 SERVINGS

In a soup pot, mix together the soup and water. Stir in the basil and garlic powder. Bring to a slow boil and then add the star noodles. Keep the slow boil going for 5 to 6 minutes or until the stars are tender.

Serve garnished with toast cut into a star shape with a cookie cutter.

GREEN STINK BUGS

2 cups orecchiette pasta

¾ cup pesto

¼ cup shredded Parmesan cheese

MAKES 4 SERVINGS

Cook the noodles according to package directions and drain; return to pan and toss with the pesto and Parmesan cheese.

THE ITALIAN WORD "ORECCHIETTE" MEANS "LITTLE EARS."

BACON CHEESEBURGER MAC

½ **pound ground beef**

1 **box Velveeta Shells & Cheese**

½ **cup cooked crumbled bacon**

1 **(14-ounce) can tomatoes, well drained**

MAKES 4 SERVINGS

In a frying pan, break up and cook the ground beef until well browned. Drain the fat and set aside the cooked meat.

Prepare the Velveeta Shells & Cheese according to the package directions, cooking the noodles for the minimum cooking time. Stir in the cooked meat, bacon, and tomatoes and heat mixture over low heat until warmed through.

FUN FACT

SYNONYMS FOR NOODLE INCLUDE AIRHEAD, BIRDBRAIN, CHUCKLEHEAD, NUMSKULL, AND SIMPLETON.

FUNKY CHICKEN SALAD

½ cup orzo

½ cup chopped celery

2 cups chopped rotisserie chicken

1 cup red grape halves

¾ cup cashew pieces

1 green onion, sliced

1 (6-ounce) container honey-flavored or plain Greek yogurt

2 to 3 tablespoons mayonnaise

Salt and pepper to taste

Bread for serving

Cook the noodles according to package directions; drain and rinse with cold water and then let cool completely. Mix together the cooled noodles with all of the remaining ingredients. Serve on a bun, croissant, soft flatbread, or pita.

MAKES 4 TO 6 SERVINGS

SWEET TREATS

GLOPPY GREEN FROG EYE SALAD

¾ **cup acini di pepe**

2 **snack-size vanilla pudding cups, chilled**

1 **small can pineapple tidbits, with juice**

1 **small can mandarin oranges, drained**

2 to 3 **cups mini marshmallows**

1 **(8-ounce) container frozen whipped topping**

Green food coloring

Large marshmallows for eyes

Green M&Ms for eyes

Vanilla frosting

Black or green licorice

Cook the noodles according to package directions; drain and let cool completely.

Combine the cooled pasta with the pudding, pineapple with juice, and oranges. Gently stir in the mini marshmallows and half of the Cool Whip. Refrigerate for 1 to 2 hours before serving. Stir the green food coloring in the remaining Cool Whip and then gently fold into salad just before serving.

To make the frog faces, create the eyes by snipping a marshmallow in half using kitchen scissors. Affix two green M&Ms using a tiny bit of frosting. Cut licorice with kitchen scissors to make mouth. Ribbit!

PASTA TRIVIA: THERE ARE AT LEAST 350 DIFFERENT NOODLE SHAPES PRODUCED WORLDWIDE!

MAKES 6 SERVINGS

CRUNCHY CINNAMON NOODLE ICE CREAM SUNDAES

½ teaspoon cinnamon

1 tablespoon brown sugar

2 tablespoons butter

1 package ramen noodles, broken into very small pieces

Vanilla ice cream

Caramel ice-cream topping

Hot fudge

Sliced bananas

Whipped cream

Maraschino cherries

In a bowl, combine the cinnamon and brown sugar and set aside. In a frying pan, melt the butter. Add the broken noodle pieces and stir with a spatula to coat. Do not use seasoning packet! Stir the cinnamon-sugar mixture into noodles to coat. Cook over warm heat a minute or two; then let cool completely.

Scoop ice cream into bowls and top with caramel, hot fudge, toasted noodles, sliced bananas, whipped cream, and maraschino cherries.

MAKES 4 TO
6 SERVINGS

SPIDER COOKIES

1 cup butterscotch or peanut butter chips

1 cup milk chocolate chips

1 (6-ounce) bag chow mein noodles

Peanuts

MAKES 16 TO 20 SERVINGS

In a large saucepan, melt both kinds of chips over low heat, stirring constantly until smooth. Stir in half of the noodles until they are completely coated. Set aside a handful of noodles to make the legs and then add the remaining noodles and stir until completely coated. Drop the mixture by the spoonful onto wax paper. Stick two peanuts onto each cookie to make the eyes. Use reserved noodles to make the legs. Let set for 45 minutes to 1 hour.

SWEET TRAIL MIX

½ teaspoon cinnamon

1 tablespoon brown sugar

2 tablespoons butter

1 package ramen noodles, broken into very small pieces

1 cup dried cherries or cranberries

1 cup dry-roasted almonds

1 king-size bag M&Ms

⅓ cup salted sunflower seed kernels

In a bowl, combine the cinnamon and brown sugar and set aside. In a frying pan, melt the butter. Add the broken noodle pieces and stir with a spatula to coat. Do not use seasoning packet! Stir the cinnamon-sugar mixture into noodles to coat. Cook over warm heat a minute or two; then let cool completely.

Add all the remaining ingredients to the crunchy cinnamon noodles in a large plastic ziplock bag and shake to combine. Enjoy!

MAKES 4 TO 6 SERVINGS

MUNCH-MUNCH CEREAL MIX

2 packages ramen noodles, broken into very small pieces

2 cups Corn Chex

1 cup regular Bugles

1 cup peanuts

¼ cup butter, melted

1 tablespoon Worcestershire sauce

¾ teaspoon seasoned salt

MAKES 6 SERVINGS

Put the noodles, Corn Chex, Bugles, and peanuts into a one-gallon plastic ziplock bag. (Do not use the ramen noodle seasoning packet!)

In a small bowl, combine the melted butter, Worcestershire sauce, and seasoned salt. Pour over the mixture in the bag, seal bag, and toss gently until it is well coated.

Line a cookie sheet with foil. Pour the mixture onto the cookie sheet and spread it out with a spatula. Bake in a preheated oven at 300 degrees F for 45 minutes. Have an adult help you stir the mixture every 15 minutes during baking. Let mix cool completely before eating. Store in an airtight container.

SUBSTITUTION CHART

IF YOU DON'T HAVE THE PASTA
LISTED ON THE LEFT, YOU CAN
SUBSTITUTE IT WITH THE
ONE LISTED ON THE RIGHT.

Acini de Pepe	Orzo or Ditalini
Angel Hair	Capellini, Vermicelli, or Thin Spaghetti
Cellentani	Cavatappi, Gemelli, or Elbow Macaroni
Chow Mein	Do not substitute
Ditalini	Canneroni or Orzo
Egg Noodles	Fettucine, Linguine, or other ribbon pasta
Elbow Macaroni	Mini Penne, Rigatoni, or Cellentani
Farfalle	Another favorite pasta
Fiori	Wheels
Fusilli	Rotini or Radiatore
Jumbo Shells	Manicotti or Cannelloni
Lasagna	Do not substitute
Manicotti	Cannelloni or Jumbo Shells
Orecchiette	Gnocchetti or Cavatelli
Orzo	Ditalini
Penne	Ziti, Rigatoni, or Elbow Macaroni
Radiatore	Rotini, Fusilli, or Spirali
Ramen	Spaghetti or Thin Spaghetti
Ravioli	Tortellini
Rigatoni	Penne, Ziti, or Elbow Macaroni
Rotini	Radiatore, Fusilli, or Spirali
Sea shells	Ditalini or Elbow Macaroni
Spaghetti	Angel Hair, Capellini, or Fettuccine
Stars	Acini de Pepe or Ditalini
Tortellini	Ravioli
Vermicelli	Angel Hair, Capellini, or Thin Spaghetti
Wheels	Fiori

INDEX

VISIT QUIRKBOOKS.COM/NOODLEMANIA TO:

See fun photos that didn't make it into the book.

Download extra recipes.

Read Q&As with the author, photographer, and illustrator.

Share your own crazy noodle photos and creations.